Shells of Hawai'i

Shells
of Hawai'i

E. Alison Kay
and
Olive Schoenberg-Dole

University of Hawaii Press
Honolulu

Unless otherwise noted, all photographs were taken by the authors.
Designed by Corinna Campbell

Library of Congress Cataloging-in-Publication Data

Kay, E. Alison, 1928-
   Shells of Hawai'i/E. Alison Kay and Olive Schoenberg-Dole.
     p.   cm.
   Includes bibliographical references (p.) and index.
   ISBN 0-8248-1316-2 (paper)
   1. Shells—Hawaii. 2. Mollusks—Hawaii. 3. Shells—Hawaii
—Identification. 4. Shells—Hawaii—Pictorial works.
I. Schoenberg-Dole, Olive, 1913-   . II. Title.
QL415.H3K39   1991
594'.0471'09969—dc20   91-2710
                                       CIP

Front cover: Achatinelline tree snails *Partulina mighelsiana*.
(Photograph by William P. Mull)

Back cover: Aplustridae, *Hydatina amplustre*. (Photograph by
S. A. Reed)

Frontispiece: Ranellidae, *Charonia tritonis,* feeding on a starfish.

Contents

The Hawaiian Archipelago

The Hawaiian Islands are the most isolated oceanic islands in the world. The Islands rose from the floor of the Pacific Ocean as sterile volcanoes and are located thousands of miles from the nearest continent. It seems quite remarkable that any living creature reached the Islands. Yet, despite its isolation, Hawai'i possesses a unique assemblage of indigenous animals and plants.

The Lovely Fleet of Islands

Mark Twain called the Hawaiian Islands "the loveliest fleet of islands that lie anchored in any ocean." The fleet, made up of 132 islands, shoals, and reefs in the mid-Pacific, is 3,486 kilometers (2,390 miles) from California, 6,196 kilometers (3,846 miles) from Japan, and 1,207 kilometers (750 miles) from the nearest small island (Figure 1). The Islands lie astride the Tropic of Cancer between 18° and 28° north of the equator and stretch for 2,451 kilometers (1,235 miles) southeast to northwest. They are anchored to the sea floor by giant volcanic pedestals.

Figure 1. Several of the Hawaiian Islands as seen from a National Aeronautics and Space Administration space shuttle. Ni'ihau and Kaua'i are in the left foreground; O'ahu, Moloka'i, Lana'i, Kaho-'olawe, and Maui near the center; and Hawai'i in the distance to the right.

1

The volcanoes that spawned the Islands may have begun as a hot spot southeast of the island of Hawai'i more than 70 million years ago. As each volcano emerged, it moved slowly northwest on the Pacific Plate, gradually eroding and sinking as it traveled. Geologists can date the birth of the Islands with some precision: Midway in the Northwestern Islands is 20 million years old; Kaua'i is built around a six-million-year-old volcano; and O'ahu is composed of two volcanoes, each of them well over two million years old. Hawai'i, the Big Island, is surprisingly young. No rocks are older than 450,000 years, and much of the island is much younger. The youngest volcano, Lō'ihi, is still more than 1,000 meters (3,281 feet) below the surface of the sea, and lies directly over the hot spot south of the island of Hawai'i.

The Hawaiian volcanoes have been gradually dissected by water and wind, which carve the fluted palis or cliffs, deep valleys, and towering sea cliffs that contribute to the Islands' spectacular scenery. The gentle climate is brought about in large part by the surrounding ocean, which acts as a giant thermostat moderating temperature. The trade winds lift the ocean air over the mountains, and as it cools, it spawns mist, clouds, and rain, which nourish abundant vegetation.

At sea level the volcanoes are fringed by coral reefs. As the Islands age, erode, and gradually disappear, the reefs remain. Indeed, in the Northwestern Islands, only the reefs remain of the volcanoes that once towered above the sea. Had it not been for coral growth, the Hawaiian Archipelago would have been approximately twelve hundred kilometers (eight hundred miles) shorter in length and would have consisted of about 28 fewer islands, banks, and shoals than it does now.

Immigrants and Descendants

The animals and plants of Hawai'i are the descendants of immigrants that came by wind and sea over miles of ocean. The ancestors of marine animals such as mollusks, corals, and fishes may have been among the first arrivals. They would have come as part of the plankton, in the form of microscopic larvae (Figure 2) in ocean currents. Some small insects and plant spores and seeds were perhaps carried across the Pacific by the same jet stream which speeds planes across the Pacific today. Small land snails, as well as sticky fruits and seeds, may have arrived on the feathers of birds.

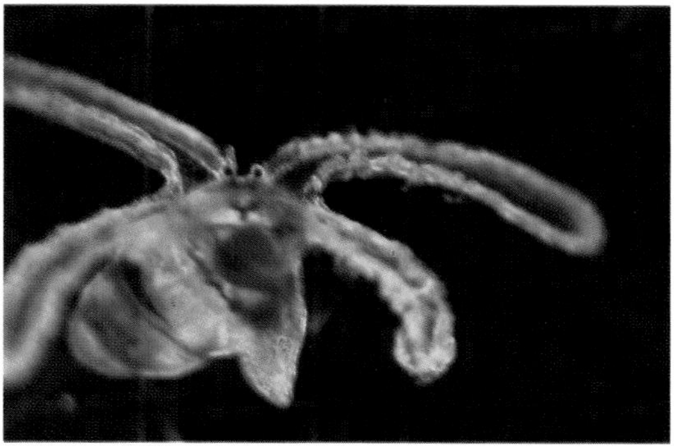

Figure 2. The planktonic veliger larva of the auger shell *Hastula strigilata* is about 900 microns (0.03 inch) long and will settle in sand when it is just over three whorls in length.

Considering the isolation of the Islands and the problem of transport, it is not surprising that whole groups of animals and plants are missing in the native biota. Neither large grazing nor browsing mammals made the journey across the Pacific Ocean. Nor were there bamboos, mangroves, abalones, giant clams, or snakes among the native animals and plants.

From the Few Many

The animals and plants that did arrive changed with time. Ancestral species of nine land snail families reached Hawai'i and, from an estimated two dozen colonizations, evolved into more than one thousand species. Thus, more than 90 percent of Hawaiian land snails are endemic, unique to the Islands.

The colonists established themselves in a new homeland with a gentle climate and an array of places to live. Perhaps even more important, they arrived without their competitors, and they left both predators and parasites at home. In the freedom of this new world, they moved into new and different habitats. Ground snails became tree dwellers. Snails that had lived in marshes moved into the damp stems of plants and under rocks. In some instances, more than two hundred species may have evolved from single colonizations.

In the ocean, evolution has been much slower. The massive speciation (appearance of new species) that occurred among the land snails did not occur in the ocean, and only about one in five of the marine mollusks is endemic, found nowhere else in the world. This difference in evolutionary rates between land and sea is the result of the nature of the two environments: the sea is a continuous medium, permitting sustained gene flow between the Islands and their neighbors, while relatively few land animals and plants can traverse the long distances. Nevertheless, there is still an interesting array of endemic species of mollusks, including three species of the limpet *Cellana* and eight species of cowries.

And Still They Come

Mollusks new to the islands continue to arrive. Before humans settled in Hawai'i, one land snail species may have colonized the Islands every 800,000 years, and a marine mollusk every 13,000 years. The immigrant Polynesians who arrived about a thousand years ago brought snails along with their plants, at a rate of perhaps one species every one hundred years. In the two hundred years since Captain Cook discovered Hawai'i for the Western world, mollusks have been introduced both accidentally and on purpose, at the rate of one species every five years. In the last 50 years alone, such well-known pests as the giant African snail (*Achatina fulica*) and the carnivorous snail (*Euglandina rosea*) have become established, along with the marine gastropod *Trochus niloticus* and the bivalve *Tapes japonica*.

An Infinite Variety

Land snails, limpets, clams, and octopuses—
pūpūkanioe, ʻopihi, ʻōlepe, and heʻe in the Hawaiian
language—are very different sorts of animals, yet
they are all included in the single word "pūpū,"
meaning "mollusk."

What Are Mollusks?

Although most mollusks are recognized by their
shells, their name derives from the Latin *mollis*
meaning "soft." Mollusks are ancient creatures, and
in the five hundred million years during which they
are known to have existed, the characteristics dis-
tinguishing them from other animals—the head,
the foot, and the body mass or visceral hump—
have become modified. These modifications have
rendered the mollusks among the most successful of
all animals. Indeed, they are second only to the
insects in number of named species in the animal
kingdom.

Mollusks occupy almost every imaginable habitat
on earth today, and some that are almost unimagin-
able. They are found in the tidal zones, exposed to
sun, rain, and waves. They bore into rocks, coral,
and wood; and they burrow into sand and mud and
into other animals. They thrive around hydrother-
mal vents at depths of more than two thousand
meters (more than six thousand feet) and at tem-
peratures of 100°C (212°F). They crawl on rocks at
sea level and on the leaves of trees 30 meters (100
feet) off the ground. Some can swim, but others are
firmly cemented to a substrate and never move at
all. Several species of snails are less than one millimeter (less than 1/32 of an inch) in diameter while the
shells of the giant clam, *Tridacna,* can reach a length
of 1.5 meters (5 feet) and can weigh as much as 272
kilograms (600 pounds). Mollusks may be among
the longest living of any invertebrate animals: at

least one bivalve, a member of the freshwater family Unionidae, has been suggested to live for at least 60 years.

From Where Did They Come?

So far, perhaps about 100,000 species of mollusks have been described worldwide, and two thousand of these species of marine and freshwater mollusks and land snails are known in Hawai'i today. They can be found from near the top of Mauna Kea 4,000 meters (13,000 feet) above sea level to depths of 305 meters (1,000 feet) below the surface of the sea around the Islands.

From where did the Hawaiian mollusks come? The marine mollusks bear an unmistakable resemblance to those found in the Pacific to the south and west of Hawai'i. Many of the land snails are also related to those found to the southwest in the Pacific, while others may be descended from land snails to the east in the Americas.

What Are Their Names?

More than two hundred mollusks bear Hawaiian names. Some of these names are rather like modern scientific names. All cowries, for example, are called leho and then further distinguished: leho nuku is the cowrie with pointed ends; leho 'ōpu'pu'u is the rough cowrie. The scientific names of these two cowries are *Cypraea cicercula* and *C. granulata;* the first term represents the genus, the second the species.

Latin names are as descriptive as the Hawaiian ones, but they may also make reference to other animals, people, or places. *Cypraea caputserpentis,* the snakehead cowrie (Figure 44), was obviously named because of the brown and white pattern of the dorsum that resembles a snake's head. *Achatinella apexfulva* (Figure 124) was given its name because of the shell's yellow tip. *Julia exquisita* is a small, green shell (Figure 99) that was named after the wife of the shell's describer, Augustus Gould. *Terebra thaanumi* (Figure 94) bears the name of a beloved malacologist of Hawai'i, Ditlev Thaanum.

The genus and the species provide names. Other relationships are indicated by larger groupings such as classes, orders, and families.

Figure 3. The triton *Cymatium intermedium* is a gastropod. Its coiled shell is covered by a hairy epidermis. It is a rock-dweller, moving about on its large foot.

Snails are officially referred to as the class Gastropoda, meaning "stomach-footed." Gastropods include mollusks with shells (Figure 3) and mollusks without shells (Figures 112–123). In shelled gastropods, the shell is usually spirally coiled and right-handed, but there are always the exceptions, and some of the land shells are left-handed (see Figure 124). Most shelled gastropods can withdraw the head and the foot into the shell by contracting a muscle attached to the central pillar or columella of the shell. In many snails the opening of the shell is closed by a horny or calcareous plug, the operculum, which is carried on the hind end of the foot (Figures 53, 61). Gastropods are found on land, in freshwater streams, and in the ocean. There are about eighteen hundred different kinds of gastropods in Hawaiʻi—one thousand on land and in freshwater streams and rivers, and the other eight hundred in the ocean.

The Bivalvia, as their name implies, have two shells (Figure 4). They are called ʻōlepe in Hawaiian, meaning "to shut and open." The valves are hinged dorsally and can be closed tightly when a pair of muscles running from one valve to the other contracts. Although bivalves have no recognizable head, they sense movement and light and darkness by means of eyespots and sensory tentacles that project between the valves. About 160 species of bivalves are known in the Islands.

There is a Hawaiian riddle that asks about a fish with eight scales. The answer is the kuapaʻa, or the

Figure 4. The pecten *Decatopecten noduliferum* is a bivalve. Its pallial tentacles are tipped with small "eyes" with a metallic blue sheen. These "eyes" serve as sensory receptors.

Figure 5. A chiton (10 mm, 0.39 inch) browses on algae on a rock in the intertidal zone.

chiton (Figure 5). Chitons, which are in the class Polyplacophora, are inconspicuous and small in Hawai'i, but they are common shore animals. The elongated, flattened body bears eight articulated plates that enable the animals to bend over the irregular surface of the rocks on which they live.

The octopus and the squid are distinguished as he'e and mūhe'e, he'e meaning "to dissolve" and mūhe'e meaning "fickle." They are in the class Cephalopoda ("head-footed"), and their ability to move backward or forward is noted by the Hawaiians who have come to describe a two-faced person

Figure 6. He'e, the day octopus, *Octopus cyanea* (4.5 kg, 10 pounds), sits near its hole on a reef in Kāne'ohe Bay. (Photograph by William van Heukelem)

as "he mūhe'e ka i'a holo lua" because "a squid is a creature that moves two ways." The most conspicuous feature of cephalopods is their arms—long, flexible, hooked, and suckered appendages that surround the mouth. The body is streamlined in squids, which are midwater animals, and saclike in octopuses (Figure 6), which live on the ocean bottom.

Living Room

When the Polynesians arrived in Hawaiʻi they must have first become familiar with the shore (kahakai) and its useful assortment of edible animals and plants. With their canoes and fishing lines they exploited the deep blue sea (kai uli) fishing for ʻōpelu, mālolo, and squid. On land they cultivated the kula lands, the sloping lands between mountain peaks and sea, and kahawai, the valleys with fresh water. Wao, the inland forest, was the source of birds and the giant koa trees from which the Hawaiians fashioned their canoes. We can similarly distinguish different kinds of habitats in which animals and plants live.

Rocky Coastlines

As lava floods into the ocean, it may create wide, flat benches of smooth basalt, or pāhoehoe. The benches vary in width and in slope, and, depending on their height above the sea, parts of them are covered and uncovered by tides twice each day. Tidal range in Hawaiʻi is about one meter (three feet). On these rocky shores, the animals and plants tend to occur in conspicuous bands or zones that are associated with tidal level (Figures 7, 8).

Above high-tide level is the splash zone. Here, sustained by spray yet tied to the sea by their sea-

Figure 7. At low tide the intertidal zone of basalt shorelines is exposed. The zone is marked by bands of colorful seaweeds.

Figure 8. The intertidal zone of the limestone bench at Kahuku, Oʻahu, is covered by an algal turf.

borne larvae, littorines (Family Littorinidae) cluster on the bare rock surface (Figure 9) at densities as high as 100,000 per square meter.

Littorines spawn only at high tide on a lunar cycle, which ensures that their eggs and sperm are carried out to sea. After perhaps 30 days in the plankton, the juvenile snails settle on shore, growing to maturity in about nine months. Small black snails, found with the littorines and seaward of them, are nerites (Family Neritidae) (Figures 32, 33), called pipipi in Hawaiian. The nerites keep their feet dry, moving up and down the shore with the tide.

Figure 9. Several pūpū kōlea, *Littorina pintado* (10 mm, 0.4 inch), cluster high on a rocky shoreline.

Figure 10. 'Opihi, *Cellana exarata* (15 mm, 0.5 inch), lift their shells above the substrate at low tide on clear, hot days.

Still farther seaward, where the shore is covered twice daily by the tides, are 'opihi, limpets (Figures 10, 31), which are among the most familiar of Hawaiian mollusks. There are two species at this level of the shore. *Cellana exarata,* makaiauli, the black foot, lives slightly higher on the shoreline than does *C. sandwicensis,* 'alinalina, the yellow foot, which is found at the water's edge at low tide. 'Opihi are well adapted to their surf-pounded habitat because their low, domed, ridged shells can deflect the force of the water and their single foot can cling so tenaciously to the rock that a 70-pound pull is necessary to break them loose. Before knives were available, 'opihi were knocked off rocks with a sharp-edged stone, and even today 'opihi-fishing is sometimes called ku'i 'opihi or 'opihi pounding. In the early years of this century, more than 68,790 kilograms (150,000 pounds) of 'opihi were sold annually in Island markets. Today only 6,879 kilograms (15,000 pounds) are marketed each year. Because of the risks involved on surfswept shores, 'opihi were known as the fish of death. At least one fisherman is lost to the sea each year while picking 'opihi.

'Opihi were 'aumakua, ancestral family gods, for some Hawaiian families. 'Opihi had two special gifts: they could defend the family from sharks by outwitting them and they could calm heavy surf. Fishermen carried 'opihi in their canoes to ensure a safe landing for their canoes.

Endemic marine mollusks (species that are found nowhere else in the world), are especially well represented on these rocky shorelines: three species of 'opihi (Figure 30), a littorine (*Nodilittorina hawaiiensis*), and the thaidids *Neothais harpa* and *Purpura aperta* (Figures 60-62) are all found only in the Hawaiian Islands.

Coral Reefs

Reefs are mosaics of corals, sand, seaweed, and solid limestone. Where reefs fringe the shore (Figure 11), the reef platform is relatively smooth, composed of variously consolidated sand, rubble, and reef rock. Much of this platform and the outer algal ridge are composed of coralline algae, and there is little living coral on the reef flats except at the seaward

Figure 11. The fringing reef at Diamond Head, O'ahu.

edge. Many of the reef communities of Hawaiʻi are subtidal, and there is dense coral growth to depths of more than 30 meters (100 feet) (Figure 12).

Coral reefs are among the most biologically productive of all natural communities. Measurements made on the island of Kauaʻi show that they yield more living material per acre than a sugarcane field. Mankind is interested in exploiting that productivity and does it by harvesting sea creatures like fishes, sea urchins, spiny lobsters, and heʻe (octopuses) that live in the reef.

Figure 12. A subtidal coral community, Kahaluʻu, Hawaiʻi, at a depth of 3 m (9.8 feet).

Octopuses live in holes on the reef flats; their lairs are advertised by piles of crab skeletons and mollusk shells. There are two species, *Octopus cyanea* or heʻe, the day "squid" (Figure 6), and *O. ornatus* or pū loa, the night "squid." There are many legends about the powers of the heʻe as well as advice on how to fish for it. One popular way to catch the octopus was to tempt it with a cowrie-shell lure. In an ancient chant, the words go: "Here is the cowrie—a red cowrie to attract the squid to his death." Cowrie shells were highly prized for their success in catching octopuses, and sometimes they were even named after a favorite grandfather or wife.

Endemic species occur in many of the families of mollusks found on the reefs. Among them are eight species of cowries (*Cypraea*) (Figures 42–47), the muricid *Chicoreus insularum* (Figure 58), the costellariid *Vexillum approximatum* (Figure 78), the strombid *Strombus vomer hawaiensis* (Figure 39) and the olive *Oliva paxillus sandwicensis* (Figure 64). Not all reef mollusks are differentiated as endemic species. Some species are only slightly different from the same species found elsewhere in the Pacific. For example, in Hawai'i the interstices of the teeth in *Cypraea caputserpentis* are brown rather than white, and the terminal blotches on *C. isabella* are brown rather than orange. Several other gastropods are distinctly larger in Hawai'i than they are elsewhere in their range. The average length of a Hawaiian tiger cowrie, *C. tigris,* is 117 millimeters (4.5 inches), while that of a tiger cowrie from the central Pacific is 77 millimeters (3 inches).

The Shifting Sand

Sand in Hawai'i comes in a variety of colors. Most of the islands are graced by curving white sand beaches but on the island of Hawai'i most beaches are of black sand or green sand. White sand is the product of coral reefs. Black sand is formed by volcanic action when, on occasion, as molten lava enters the ocean, steam explosions produce volcanic glass and cinders. Green sand is made of olivines that have been washed from basalt and become concentrated on some shorelines. Sand, whether of calcareous or volcanic origin, is a soft, shifting, and somewhat unstable habitat; but it has been exploited by both gastropods and bivalves. Gastropods that live in sand have many curious adaptations, among them the remarkable versatility of the foot.

The terebrid *Hastula hectica* (Figure 13) lives on sand beaches where the waves break. It is an extraordinarily agile animal. When a swell passes over

Figure 13. The terebrid, or auger shell, *Hastula hectica* (30 mm, 1.2 inches) burrows in sand on a beach.

the buried terebrid, the animal crawls to the surface, flips over, sails seaward in the backwash with the foot acting as a sail, digs into the sand where it feeds on worms, and remains buried in the sand until the next wave passes over it.

Subtidal sand, that below the low-tide mark, is intricately marked by the trails made by burrowing animals (Figure 14). Two of the largest gastropods in Hawai'i, the helmet shell, *Cassis cornuta,* and the tun shell, *Tonna perdix* (Figure 50), plow wide tracks in the sand. Smaller sand dwellers, *Oliva* and *Conus,* carve narrower trails (Figure 14). In the moon shells (Family Naticidae) (Figures 48, 49), the foot not only serves as a plow when the naticid moves through the sand, but it also expands, cover-

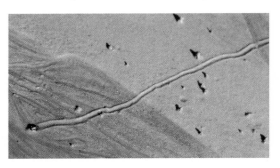

Figure 14. Olive shells make conspicuous trails in subtidal sand.

ing the shell and protecting the mantle cavity from siltation. The foot is almost infinitely expansible and can be blown up like a balloon by water moving into cavities in the tissues.

The most distinctive mode of locomotion among sand dwellers is that of strombids, which have a strong, pointed foot to which is attached a sharp, sometimes serrated operculum. The operculum acts as a lever, and when strombids move they do so with short, jerky jumps. Specimens of *Strombus maculatus* move about 1.1 centimeters per minute, with nearly two leaps each minute. When a preda-tory cone is nearby, the strombids have been seen to leap more than a meter.

The Life of the Open Sea

Each year when the prevailing trade winds return (after a period of calm brought about by southerly winds) the beaches of the main islands are often

Figure 15. The aeolid nudibranch *Glaucus atlanticus* has winglike appendages that match the colors of the open sea.

Figure 16. The purple snail *Janthina* floats on a cushion of air bubbles.

strewn with dead and dying animals tossed up by the waves. Among these animals are siphonophores, like the Portuguese man-of-war, *Physalia;* the purple snail, *Janthina;* and the pelagic nudibranch, *Glaucus.* The latter two are carnivorous, feeding on *Physalia* and other coelenterates. *Glaucus* (Figure 15) stays afloat by gulping air and holding a bubble inside the stomach. *Janthina* secretes a float of air bubbles (Figure 16) on which it deposits rows of egg capsules. In both *Janthina* and *Glaucus,* the animals are darker colored on the dorsal surface and silver or white on the underside.

The mollusks of the open sea are cosmopolitan, found in all of the world's oceans.

Rivers to the Sea

The Kumulipo, the Hawaiian creation chant, tells of life moving out of the oceans and into freshwater streams and then on to land. The hīhīwai or wī, the neritid *Neritina granosa* (Family Neritidae) (Figure 17), of freshwater streams is singled out as the connecting link between land and sea.

The hīhīwai has one of the most remarkable life cycles of any of the Hawaiian mollusks. It is diadromous like the salmon, able to live both in fresh water and in the ocean. Adult hīhīwai live in streams and deposit their eggs in tough capsules attached to shells or rocks. Within 30 days, hundreds of larvae hatch and are carried downstream and out to sea. Some weeks later, tiny snails only a millimeter (¹⁄₃₂ of an inch) long invade the mouths of streams and begin to move upstream. These gas-

Figure 17. Hīhīwai, *Neritina granosa* (30 mm, 1.2 inches), with granular shells are found near the mouths of streams. Egg capsules often are attached to the shells. (Photograph by John Ford)

tropods are apparently even able to climb waterfalls and have been found at elevations of 366 meters (1,200 feet). The sculpture on the shell reflects their habitat: snails living near the mouths of streams have wide, granular shells; those living upstream have smooth, narrow shells.

The hīhīwai and five or six other fresh water gastropods are endemic to Hawai'i.

Snails in Trees

Early in the nineteenth century, a visiting explorer who, during his travels around the world had encountered "horrible amphibians and numberless insects" in tropical forests, wrote that on O'ahu, "if you shake the trees, instead of insects falling off, there are prettily shaped, often brightly colored snails." The snails he described were the achatinellines (subfamily Achatinellinae), the tree snails (Figures 18, 124, 125). In Hawaiian these snails are called pupukanioe, "the shell that sounds long," because they were thought to sing as they crawled up and down the trees. Less romantic scholars suggest that those soft night songs of the forests are made by crickets.

The ancestral achatinellines exploited the trees of Oʻahu, Maui, Molokaʻi, and Lanaʻi, evolving into an array of colorful shells. Achatinellines spend their entire lives in trees. They graze on fungi or spores

Figure 18. Achatinelline tree snails give birth to living young, one at a time and only about one a year. This achatinelline is *Partulina mighelsiana* from Maui. (Photograph by William P. Mull)

that grow on the leaves, rather than eating the leaves themselves. These snails give birth to living young, retaining the eggs inside the body until they hatch as crawling juveniles. Adult achatinellines are slow-moving, and the same colony has been seen in one tree over periods of several years. Their low mobility and their isolation on mountain ridges were apparently the right recipe for the evolution of the large number of species.

Land shells were collected by the thousands during the nineteenth century and the first decades of the twentieth century. These enormous collections, together with the destruction of habitat and the introduction of predators such as rats and the carnivorous snail *Euglandina rosea*, have led to their virtual extinction today.

In answer to the question "What do animals spend their time doing?" a wise biologist replied, "Mostly nothing, but when they do something, they mostly eat."

Snails' Teeth

The familiar way in which food is handled among animals is by teeth. In gastropods and chitons, teeth are part of the radula, a structure unique to mollusks. In its simplest form, the radula consists of numerous teeth attached to a membranous ribbon (Figures 19, 20). A part of this ribbon is protruded through the mouth and is moved across a surface, scraping encrusting organisms into the mouth. As with all molluscan parts, the radula has evolved in various ways: in some forms there are hundreds of teeth in a row; in others there are only a few teeth. In the predatory cones and other toxoglossans, there is but a single tooth. Within this range of structure radular teeth can scrape, grasp and bite, probe, bore holes through shells, or act as a highly efficient harpoon.

'Opihi scrape diatoms from their rock homes with a narrow radula consisting of only two robust, sicklelike teeth in each row (Figure 20). The radula is a cutting tool in the sea hare, *Aplysia,* which might

Figure 19. The cowrie *Cypraea tigris* feeds by moving the radula, here protruding from the mouth, across the surface of rocks. The siphon, mantle papillae, and the tentacles frame the mouth and proboscis.

Figure 20. Scanning electron micrographs of radulae of some Hawaiian mollusks. 1. Partial radular ribbon of an 'opihi, *Cellana sandwicensis*. 2. Partial radular ribbon of *Mitra mitra*. 3. Partial radular ribbon of a cowrie, *Cypraea semiplota*. 4. The radular ribbon on a coral-feeding muricacean, *Drupella* sp. (Bars = 100 micrometers [1/10th of a millimeter = 0.003937 in.]).

better be called a sea cow because it feeds, for example, by grasping sea lettuce, *Ulva,* with the radula, cutting off chunks with the jaws, and then grinding it in the gizzard. Sacoglossans, shell-less opisthobranchs (Figures 112–114), have a single tooth in each radular row. The tooth slits algal cells from which the mollusk pumps the cell contents.

Molluscan predators are equally specialized. The moon shells *Natica* and *Polinices* and some muricaceans seize and hold their molluscan prey with

Figure 21. *Epitonium ulu* feed on the mushroom coral *Fungia*. Shells of *Epitonium* are about 10 mm (0.4 inch) long; the coral is about 30 cm (12 inches) long.

Figure 22. Eulimid gastropods (9 mm, 0.35 inch) feeding on a sea cucumber.

the foot, pressing the proboscis against the victim's shell and drilling a neat, round feeding hole with the radula (Figure 24). The tun shell, *Tonna perdix,* stalks its holothurian (sea cucumber) prey with the siphon extended, then engulfs it with the proboscis. The secretion of sulphuric acid by the buccal glands helps to soften the hapless sea cucumber.

The most notorious of molluscan predators are the cones which attack their prey with a barbed tooth shot out like an arrow. The venom is a neurotoxin and paralyzes the prey. It can also be harmful to the unwary human shell collector. Most cones eat worms, but a few specialize on mollusks (Figure 23) and fish. The prey may be as large as the predator, but it is broken down by powerful digestive enzymes. After feeding on its prey, the cone withdraws into its shell.

Parasites are predators that live on or within the body of a living host. They do not kill their hosts or they themselves would die. Molluscan parasites are always much smaller than their hosts. The gastropod that feeds on the mushroom coral *Fungia* is ¹⁄₁₀ the size of its host (Figure 21), and those that parasitize the sea cucumber *Holothuria atra* are ¹⁄₁₀₀ the length of their hosts (Figure 22). These parasites feed by sucking tissue from their hosts.

'Ewa's Silent Sea Creature

Bivalves have no head and no teeth (Figures 4, 25). Their food consists of microscopic particles suspended in the water. These particles are filtered out

Figure 23. *Conus textile* feeds on other mollusks, including the cone *Conus ebraeus.*

Figure 24. The shell of a pipipi, *Nerita picea* (14 mm, 0.5 inch) drilled by the muricacean *Neothais harpa* (28 mm, 1.1 inches).

by the gills as large quantities of water—as much as three liters (three quarts) an hour—are pumped in at one end of the animal and out the other. When the valves are open, the animals are feeding. When they are closed, the animals have shut down for a while.

Pearl Harbor was named after the pipi (Figure 25), the pearl oyster that once lived within its shal-

Figure 25. Seawater with microscopic food particles is pumped through the partially open valves of 'Ewa's silent sea creature, the pearl oyster, *Pinctada margaritifera*.

low waters. It was well known that the pipi would close up tight and vanish if they were disturbed. Thus, when people gathered pipi they were very quiet about it. Sounds would cause breezes, which in turn caused ripples on the surface of the water, and the pipi would disappear. For this reason pipi were known as "i'a hāmau leo o 'Ewa" ('Ewa's silent sea creature), although it was not the pipi that were silent but the people who gathered them!

The Numbers Game

In *The Origin of Species,* Charles Darwin wrote, "There is no exception to the rule that every organic being increases at so high a rate, that, if not destroyed, the earth would be covered by the progeny of a single pair."

The Prodigal and the Prudent

That some marine animals produce astronomical numbers of eggs is well known. Hawaiian mollusks are no exception (Figure 26-A, B). *Conus quercinus* may spawn 336,500 eggs each year and 3,700,000 in a lifetime. The sea hare, *Aplysia juliana,* may produce two million eggs in its six-month life span. A female *Littorina pintado* spawns nearly 500,000 eggs if she lives her allotted lifetime of six years. Other numbers are less spectacular but still substantial: *Conus pennaceus* may spawn 4,000 eggs a year (Figure 89), 39,000 in its lifetime; and *Octopus cyanea* may produce 1,200 embryos.

Reproductive sweepstakes are played not only by the prodigal but by the prudent. The prudent mollusk produces very few offspring. The consumate strategist in this game is the land snail, *Achatinella mustelina,* which has but a single keiki (baby) a year.

Figure 26. Hundreds of eggs are deposited in the colorful egg capsules of A) *Vitularia miliaris* and B) *Fusinus undatus.*

Despite this numbers game, it turns out that the way an animal breeds may have very little to do with how many there are. The simple facts are that 99.9 percent of the sea hare's eggs never reach maturity, and that when *Aplysia* (Figures 109–111) are counted on a reef there are only three or four per square meter and often none at all. Yet counts of tree snails in Hawai'i at the beginning of the century indicate at least five hundred snails, and perhaps as many as two thousand in a single tree.

Ecologists suggest that different life history strategies fit different environments. Where food or space or climate fluctuates, production of as many offspring as possible ensures that some will survive the almost inevitable catastrophe. Species that live in stable environments do better with a few well-developed young. Before humans reached Hawai'i, *Achatinella* lived in a benign environment with few or no predators.

The prodigal not only produce many young, but the young are small and mature rapidly. Many reproduce only once. *Aplysia juliana* matures about 90 days after hatching; its average life span is about six months. *Octopus cyanea* is mature within about 10 months, produces one batch of eggs, and dies within 10 days of the last egg hatching. The young of the prudent are large. They mature late. They live a long time and reproduce several times. The juveniles of achatinellines (Figure 18), which emerge from the parent mantle cavity, are 4.5 mm long, about one-fourth the length of the parent. They mature at six years, and they may live for 11 years.

Pyramids of Numbers

Reproductive strategies ensure the survival of the species; the community in which organisms live determines abundance.

Communities can be likened to pyramids. At the base is a multitude of microscopic plants and animals. They support a smaller number of larger creatures. At the top are even fewer animals. A pyramid of this type can be seen on any rocky shoreline merely by counting the numbers of the various kinds of animals present. On the shoreline bench at Diamond Head, O'ahu, there are about 25,000

Figure 27. The carnivorous gastropod *Morula granulata* (21 mm, 0.8 inch) feeding on the minute vermetid *Dendropoma gregaria* (2 mm, 0.08 inch) on the intertidal bench at Diamond Head, O'ahu.

small bivalves (*Brachidontes crebristriatus*) per square meter (1.2 square yards) and another 10,000 small worm shells (*Dendropoma gregaria*). Both the bivalves and the worm shells feed on microscopic plants in the plankton. In turn, their shells are drilled, and they are eaten by the thaidid *Morula granulata* (Figure 27), of which there are only about three per square meter.

The common mollusks are near the base of the pyramid. They are small, abundant, and feed on photosynthetic plants that form the pyramid base. The mollusks toward the top of the pyramid are larger and relatively few in number, and they are carnivores.

Shells in History

Mollusks have perhaps played a more important part in relation to humans in Hawai'i than have any other animal group. Archaeological middens are mute testimony to the role of mollusks in the early economy of the Islands. Mollusks were important not only as food but as tools, and were also used as fish hooks, domestic utensils, musical instruments, and ornaments (Figure 28).

When Westerners arrived, among the first things they looked for were shells. Among the shells taken back to London on the first voyage that discovered Hawai'i for the Western world in 1778 was a specimen of the kūpe'e, the painted nerite, *Nerita polita* (Family Neritidae; Figure 32). The shell was sold at auction in London in 1806 for nine guineas, the same price paid at the same auction for a feather cloak. When a feather cloak was sold a few years ago, it fetched $150,000; the kūpe'e sells today for 10 cents.

In the middle of the nineteenth century, many schoolboys caught a disease their parents called "the shell fever." The boys took to spending their weekends and holidays hiking in the mountains, where they collected thousands of land shells. Many of these collections now serve as unique source material for evolutionary study.

The hard, calcareous shells of mollusks are often preserved as fossils. Marine fossils are common in the fossil reefs of Midway, O'ahu, Moloka'i, and Maui and provide insight into the geological history of the island chain. Fossil land shells, in several deposits and from archaeological middens, are providing clues about the relationship between the ancient Hawaiians and their environment.

Figure 28. Shell leis made on the island of Ni'ihau are strung with tiny turbinid and columbellid shells and are popular items of jewelry.

Success or Extinction?

Mollusks are considered to be among the most successful of all animals, although success is a relative term. With few exceptions, all creatures are prey to other creatures. The animal that survives long enough to breed is successful. All else is failure.

There have been many failures among the animals and plants of Hawai'i. The fossil record as we know it today is not complete, but the fossil mollusks of which we have record suggest that perhaps one species per million years became extinct before the Islands were inhabited by humans (Figure 29).

Figure 29. The giant oyster, *Pycnodonta kamehameha* (20 cm, 7.8 inches), was endemic to the Hawaiian Islands but is extinct; it evolved during the Pleistocene ice ages.

The fossils that are contemporaneous with mankind tell a different story. If the land snails in archaeological middens and cultural layers that appear to have become extinct during Polynesian habitation are representative, then an extinction rate of one species every one hundred years during the prehistoric period becomes a possibility. With the coming of Westerners, the extinction rate has again increased. Of the 41 known species of *Achatinella* on O'ahu alone, more than half have become extinct in the last 50 years. If, as has been suggested, virtually all the native ground-living land snails are also extinct today, then in the two hundred years that Westerners have been in Hawai'i the extinction rate is about three species a year.

*Protection for a
Unique Biota*

The shells of Hawai'i are unique. A few immigrant mollusks arrived by chance in these oceanic islands, and over millions of years they have undergone evolutionary change. Ocean barriers, channels between islands, and valleys and ridges within islands have restricted gene flow, which, together with an astonishing diversity of habitat, has resulted in remarkable evolutionary novelties—marine limpets, fresh water nerites, and tree snails. But, while unique assemblages of mollusks on land and in the sea have provided the opportunities for evolutionary experiments, these same oceanic island communities are delicately balanced and easily disturbed. Introductions of alien snails and other animals and plants, and growing human population pressures that bring exploitation, over-fishing, and the destruction of habitat are rapidly depriving the world of an extraordinary biota.

Few of the mollusks of Hawai'i currently have any degree of protection. All members of the genus *Achatinella* are recognized as endangered species by federal law, the only instance where a genus and not just a single species is protected. Following the exploitation in the 1920s of the only pearl oyster bed known to exist in the Hawaiian Islands, that at Pearl and Hermes Reef, a law was enacted that forbids collection of specimens of the pearl oyster *Pinctada margaritifera* in the Hawaiian Archipelago. The three species of 'opihi (*Cellana exarata, C. sandwicensis,* and *C. talcosa*) and he'e (*Octopus cyanea* and *O. ornatus*) are fished commercially. Because of dwindling stocks, size regulations have been imposed for 'opihi and octopuses. No 'opihi less than 33 mm (1¼ inches) in shell length may be harvested, and octopuses must weigh 0.45 kilograms (one pound) before they can be caught for commercial purposes.

We need only remember that it was Charles Darwin's visit to a Pacific island group, the Galapagos, and his recognition of a unique biota in that archipelago that sparked one of the greatest revolutions in thought of all time. One can but wonder if an equally significant idea might yet be spawned from the Hawaiian biota should it survive.

Species

We illustrate more than three hundred species of Hawaiian mollusks. Although shells are prized by many collectors for their jewellike quality, few shells are found as perfect specimens in nature, and some of the shells we have illustrated are blemished.

Figure 30.
Patellidae:
1. *Cellana sandwicensis*
(Pease, 1861), 35 mm;
2. *Cellana exarata*
(Reeve, 1854), 30 mm;
3. *Cellana talcosa*
(Gould, 1846), 80 mm.
Trochidae:
4. *Trochus intextus*
Kiener, 1850, 30 mm.
Turbinidae:
5. *Turbo sandwicensis*
Pease, 1861, 35 mm.

Figure 31.
Patellidae:
Cellana sandwicensis
(Pease, 1861), 30 mm.
(Photograph by James
O'Neil)

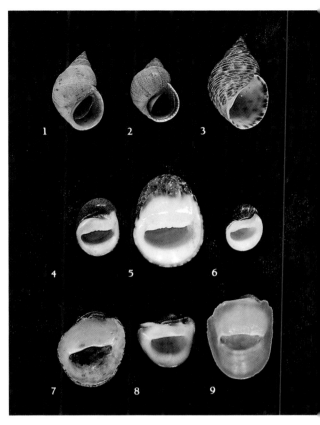

Figure 32.
Littorinidae:
1. *Littorina undulata*
Gray, 1839, 24 mm;
2. *Littorina pintado*
(Wood, 1828), 20 mm;
3. *Littorina scabra*
(Linnaeus, 1758),
27 mm.
Neritidae:
4. *Nerita picea*
(Récluz, 1841), 20 mm;
5. *Nerita polita*
Linnaeus, 1758, 30 mm;
6. *Theodoxus neglectus*
(Pease, 1861), 15 mm;
7. *Neritina granosa*
Sowerby, 1825, 27 mm;
8. *Theodoxus cariosus*
(Wood, 1828), 20 mm;
9. *Theodoxus vespertinus*
(Sowerby, 1849),
30 mm.

Figure 33.
Neritidae:
Nerita picea
(Récluz, 1841), in situ,
15 mm.

Figure 34.
Cerithiidae:
1. *Cerithium rostratum*
Sowerby, 1855, 20 mm;
2. *Cerithium nesioticum*
Pilsbry and Vanatta,
1905, 15 mm.
3. *Cerithium
atromarginatum*
Dautzenberg and
Bouge, 1933, 10 mm.
Planaxidae:
4. *Planaxis labiosa*
A. Adams, 1853,
10 mm.
Eulimidae:
5. *Balcis bryani*
Pilsbry, 1917, 15 mm;
6. *Balcis thaanumi*
(Pilsbry, 1917), 30 mm;
7. *Balcis cumingii*
(A. Adams, 1854),
24 mm.
Epitoniidae:
8. *Epitonium perplexum*
(Déshayes, 1863),
25 mm.
Modulidae:
9. *Modulus tectum*
(Gmelin, 1791), 15 mm.

Figure 35.
Vermetidae:
Serpulorbis variabilis
Hadfield and Kay, 1972,
in situ, 25 mm.

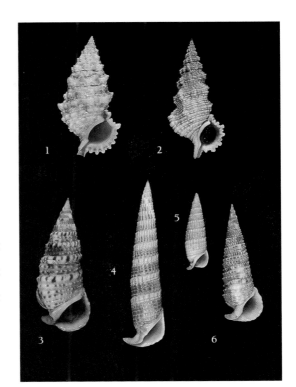

Figure 36.
Cerithiidae:
1. *Cerithium mutatum*
Sowerby, 1834, 40 mm;
2. *Cerithium columna*
Sowerby, 1834, 40 mm;
3. *Rhinoclavis sinensis*
(Gmelin, 1791), 50 mm;
4, 5. *Rhinoclavis fasciata*
(Bruguiére, 1792),
55 mm, 25 mm;
6. *Rhinoclavis articulata*
(Adams and Reeve,
1850), 40 mm.

Figure 37.
Cerithiidae:
Bittium zebrum
(Kiener, 1841), 6 mm.

Figure 38.
Strombidae:
1. *Strombus dentatus*
Linnaeus, 1758, 45 mm;
2. *Strombus helli*
Kiener, 1843, 25 mm;
3. *Strombus maculatus*
Sowerby, 1842, 28 mm;
4. *Strombus vomer*
hawaiensis
Pilsbry, 1917, 70 mm.

Figure 39.
Strombidae:
Strombus vomer
hawaiensis
Pilsbry, 1917: two ani-
mals with the eyes
visible in the strom-
boid notch, 65 mm.

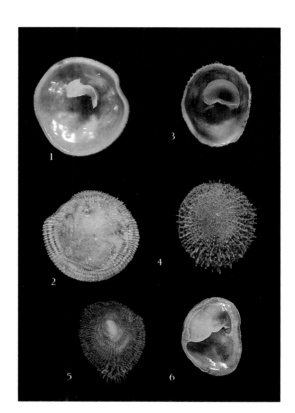

Figure 40.
Calyptraeidae:
1, 2. *Cheilea equestris*
(Linnaeus, 1758),
30 mm;
3, 4. *Crucibulum spinosum*
(Sowerby, 1824),
25 mm.
Hipponicidae:
5. *Hipponix pilosus*
(Déshayes, 1832),
20 mm.
Calyptraeidae:
6. *Crepidula aculeata*
(Gmelin, 1791), 25 mm.

Figure 41.
Hipponicidae:
Sabia conica
(Schumacher, 1817),
9 mm. on the nassariid
Nassarius papillosus
(Linnaeus, 1758),
40 mm.

35

Figure 42.
Cypraeidae:
1. *Cypraea talpa*
Linnaeus, 1758, 65 mm.
2. *Cypraea leviathan*
Schilder and Schilder,
1937, 65 mm.
3. *Cypraea maculifera*
Schilder, 1932, 58 mm.
4. *Cypraea mauritiana*
Linnaeus, 1758, 85 mm.

Figure 43.
Cypraeidae:
Cypraea talpa
Linnaeus, 1758, 65 mm.

Figure 44.
Cypraeidae:
1. *Cypraea caputserpentis*
Linnaeus, 1758, 32 mm;
2. *Cypraea moneta*
Linnaeus, 1758, 25 mm;
3. *Cypraea helvola*
Linnaeus, 1758, 20 mm;
4. *Cypraea poraria*
Linnaeus, 1758, 15 mm;
5. *Cypraea mauiensis*
Burgess, 1967, 12 mm;
6. *Cypraea teres*
Gmelin, 1791, 35 mm;
7. *Cypraea rashleighana*
Melvill, 1888, 22 mm;
8. *Cypraea alisonae*
Burgess, 1983, 32 mm.

Figure 45.
Cypraeidae:
Cypraea tigris
Linnaeus, 1758,
100 mm.

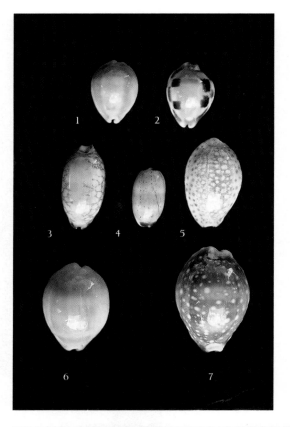

Figure 46.
Cypraeidae:
1. *Cypraea schilderorum*
(Iredale, 1939), 33 mm;
2. *Cypraea tessellata*
Swainson, 1822,
35 mm;
3. *Cypraea scurra*
Gmelin, 1791, 45 mm;
4. *Cypraea isabella*
Linnaeus, 1758, 32 mm;
5. *Cypraea chinensis*
Gmelin, 1791, 47 mm;
6. *Cypraea sulcidentata*
Gray, 1824, 48 mm;
7. *Cypraea vitellus*
Linnaeus, 1758, 58 mm.

Figure 47.
Cypraeidae:
Cypraea schilderorum
(Iredale, 1939), female
on its egg mass, 30mm.
(Photograph by Mike
Severns)

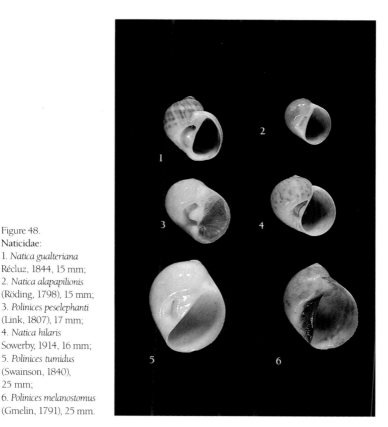

Figure 48.
Naticidae:
1. *Natica gualteriana*
Récluz, 1844, 15 mm;
2. *Natica alapapilionis*
(Röding, 1798), 15 mm;
3. *Polinices peselephanti*
(Link, 1807), 17 mm;
4. *Natica hilaris*
Sowerby, 1914, 16 mm;
5. *Polinices tumidus*
(Swainson, 1840),
25 mm;
6. *Polinices melanostomus*
(Gmelin, 1791), 25 mm.

Figure 49.
Naticidae:
Polinices tumidus (Swain-
son, 1840), 25 mm.

Figure 50.
Cassididae:
1. *Casmaria ponderosa*
(Gmelin, 1791), 40 mm;
2. *Casmaria erinaceus
kalosmodix*
(Melvill, 1883), 55 mm;
3. *Phalium umbilicatum*
(Pease, 1861), 35 mm.
Tonnidae:
4. *Tonna perdix*
(Linnaeus, 1758),
65 mm;
5. *Malea pomum*
(Linnaeus, 1758),
65 mm.

Figure 51.
Cassididae:
Casmaria ponderosa
(Gmelin, 1791), 45 mm.
depositing egg capsules.

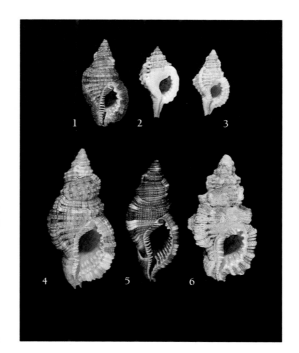

Figure 52.
Ranellidae:
1. *Cymatium
intermedium*
(Pease, 1869), 60 mm;
2. *Cymatium muricinum*
(Röding, 1798), 45 mm;
3. *Cymatium gemmatum*
(Reeve, 1844), 45 mm;
4. *Cymatium aquatile*
(Reeve, 1844), 90 mm;
5. *Cymatium pileare*
(Linnaeus, 1758),
90 mm;
6. *Cymatium
nicobaricum*
(Röding, 1798), 80 mm.

Figure 53.
Ranellidae:
Charonia tritonis
(Linnaeus, 1758),
255 mm, feeding
on a starfish.
(Photograph by Mike
Severns)

41

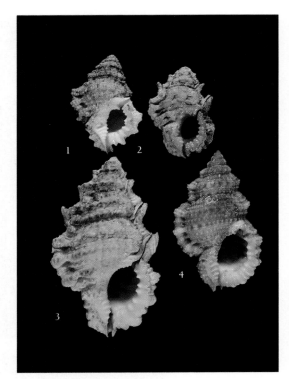

Figure 54.
Bursidae:
1. *Bursa cruentata*
(Sowerby, 1841),
45 mm;
2. *Bursa rosa*
(Perry, 1811), 45 mm;
3. *Bursa bufonia*
(Gmelin, 1791), 75 mm;
4. *Bursa granularis*
(Röding, 1798), 60 mm.

Figure 55.
Ranellidae:
Distorsio anus
Linnaeus, 1758, 60 mm.

Figure 56.
Architectonicidae:
1, 2, 3. *Architectonica perspectiva* (Linnaeus, 1758), 32 and 35 mm;
4, 5. *Philippia oxytropis* A. Adams, 1855, 15 mm.
Xenophoridae:
6, 7. *Xenophora peroniana* (Iredale, 1929), 40 mm.

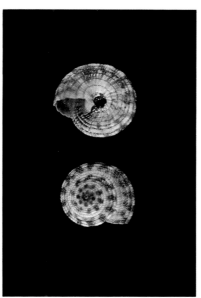

Figure 57.
Architectonicidae:
Heliacus variegatus (Gmelin, 1791), 12 mm.

Figure 58.
Muricidae:
1. *Homalocantha
anatomica*
(Perry, 1811), 55 mm;
2. *Chicoreus insularum*
(Pilsbry, 1921), 90 mm.

Figure 59.
Muricidae:
Marchia martinetana
(Röding, 1798), 45 mm,
showing foot and
siphon.

Figure 60.
Thaididae:
1. *Drupa ricina*
(Linnaeus, 1758),
25 mm;
2. *Drupa grossularia*
(Röding, 1798), 25 mm;
3. *Drupa rubusidaeus*
(Röding, 1798), 40 mm;
4. *Drupa morum*
(Röding, 1798), 40 mm;
5. *Purpura aperta*
(Blainville, 1832),
75 mm;
6. *Thais armigera*
(Link, 1807), 65 mm.

Figure 61.
Thaididae:
Purpura aperta
(Blainville, 1832), 50
mm, attacking an 'opihi
with foot and oper-
culum at the edge of the
'opihi shell.

Figure 62.
Thaididae:
1. *Morula uva*
(Röding, 1798), 18 mm;
2. *Morula granulata*
(Duclos, 1832), 16 mm;
3. *Morula dumosa*
(Conrad, 1837), 18 mm;
4. *Drupella* sp.,
25 mm.
Muricidae:
5. *Vitularia miliaris*
(Gmelin, 1791), 18 mm.
Thaididae:
6. *Pinaxia versicolor*
(Gray, 1839), 25 mm.
Muricidae:
7. *Muricodrupa funiculus*
(Wood, 1828), 17 mm.
Thaididae:
8. *Neothais harpa*
(Conrad, 1837), 25 mm;
9. *Morula foliacea*
(Conrad, 1837), 22 mm;
10. *Thais intermedia*
(Kiener, 1836), 35 mm;
11. *Nassa serta*
(Bruguiére, 1789),
35 mm;
12. *Drupella elata*
Blainville, 1832, 30 mm.

Figure 63.
Coralliophilidae:
Magilopsis lamarckii
(Déshayes, 1863),
20 mm, in its burrow in
coral.

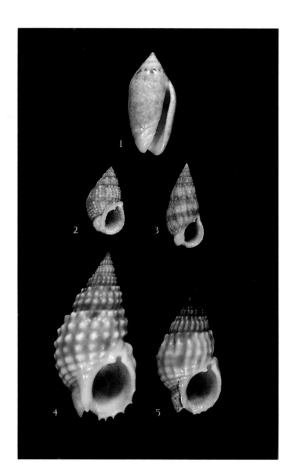

Figure 64.
Olividae:
1. *Oliva paxillus sandwicensis*
Pease, 1860, 27 mm.
Nassariidae:
2. *Nassarius crematus*
(Hinds, 1844), 20 mm;
3. *Nassarius gaudiosus*
(Hinds, 1844), 20 mm;
4. *Nassarius papillosus*
(Linnaeus, 1758),
45 mm;
5. *Nassarius hirtus*
(Kiener, 1834), 34 mm.

Figure 65.
Nassariidae:
Nassarius pauperus
(Gould, 1850), 6 mm.

Figure 66.
Columbellidae:
1. *Euplica turturina*
(Lamarck, 1822),
12 mm;
2. *Euplica livescens*
(Reeve, 1859), 12 mm.
Fasciolariidae:
3. *Peristernia chlorostoma*
(Sowerby, 1825),
15 mm.
Buccinidae:
4. *Cantharus farinosus*
(Gould, 1850), 12 mm;
5. *Phos roseatus*
(Hinds, 1844), 18 mm.
Buccinidae:
6. *Clivipollia costata*
(Pease, 1860), 20 mm;
7. *Prodotia iostomus*
(Gray *in* Griffiths and
Pidgeon, 1834), 20 mm;
8. *Prodotia ignea*
(Gmelin, 1791), 20 mm.

Figure 67.
Buccinidae:
Engina albocincta
Pease, 1860, 6 mm.

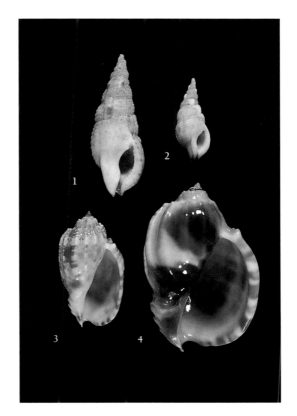

Figure 68.
Colubrariidae:
1. *Colubraria obscura*
(Reeve, 1844), 55 mm;
2. *Colubraria tortuosa*
(Reeve, 1844), 33 mm.
Harpidae:
3. *Harpa amouretta*
Röding, 1798, 48 mm;
4. *Harpa major*
Röding, 1798, 65 mm.

Figure 69.
Harpidae:
Harpa harpa (Linnaeus,
1758), showing foot,
siphon, and tentacles,
50 mm.

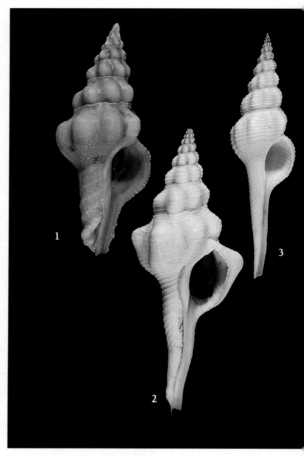

Figure 70.
Fasciolariidae:
1. *Latirus nodatus*
(Gmelin, 1791), 60 mm;
2. *Fusinus* sp., 105 mm;
3. *Fusinus sandvicensis*
(Sowerby, 1880),
95 mm.

Figure 71.
Fasciolariidae:
Latirus noumeensis
(Crosse, 1870), 10 mm.

Figure 72.
Mitridae:
1. *Mitra mitra*
(Linnaeus, 1758),
120 mm;
2. *Mitra incompta*
(Solander *in* Lightfoot,
1786), 85 mm;
3. *Mitra papalis*
(Linnaeus, 1758),
100 mm.

Figure 73.
Mitridae:
Mitra typha
Reeve, 1845, 10 mm.

Figure 74.
Mitridae:
1. *Mitra litterata*
Lamarck, 1811, 21 mm;
2. *Mitra coronata*
Lamarck, 1811, 20 mm;
3. *Mitra pellisserpentis*
Reeve, 1844, 25 mm;
4. *Mitra fulvescens*
Broderip, 1836, 28 mm;
5. *Mitra ticaonica*
Reeve, 1844, 26 mm;
6. *Mitra assimilis*
Pease, 1868, 22 mm;
7. *Mitra coffea*
Schubert and Wagner,
1829, 40 mm;
8. *Mitra ferruginea*
Lamarck, 1811, 40 mm;
9. *Mitra stictica*
(Link, 1807), 40 mm.

Figure 75.
Mitridae:
Mitra stictica
(Link, 1807), 35mm,
with siphon showing.

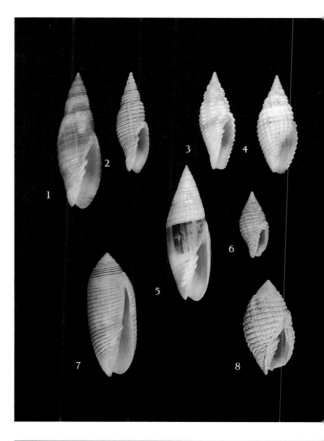

Figure 76.
Mitridae:
1. *Neocancilla clathrus*
(Gmelin, 1791), 30 mm;
2. *Cancilla granatina*
(Lamarck, 1811),
20 mm;
3. *Subcancilla foveolata*
(Dunker, 1858), 20 mm;
4. *Neocancilla papilio
langfordi*
J. Cate, 1962, 18 mm;
5. *Scabricola newcombi*
(Pease, 1869), 28 mm;
6. *Mitra avenacea*
Reeve, 1845, 15 mm;
7. *Pterygia crenulata*
(Gmelin, 1791), 28 mm;
8. *Pterygia pudica*
(Pease, 1860), 20 mm.

Figure 77.
Mitridae:
Imbricaria olivaeformis
(Swainson, 1821),
15mm, in sand with
siphons showing.

Figure 78.
Costellariidae:
1. *Vexillum lautum*
(Reeve, 1845), 15 mm;
2. *Vexillum patriarchalis*
(Gmelin, 1791), 10 mm;
3. *Vexillum tuberosum*
(Reeve, 1845), 12 mm;
4. *Vexillum unifasciatum*
(Wood, 1828), 25 mm;
5. *Vexillum pacificum*
(Reeve, 1845), 12 mm;
6. *Vexillum xenium*
(Pilsbry, 1921), 22 mm;
7. *Vexillum*
approximatum
(Pease, 1860), 30 mm;
8. *Vexillum*
cancellarioides
(Anton, 1839), 18 mm;
9. *Vexillum interstriatum*
(Sowerby, 1870),
25 mm;
10. *Vexillum*
macrospirum
(A. Adams, 1853),
30 mm.

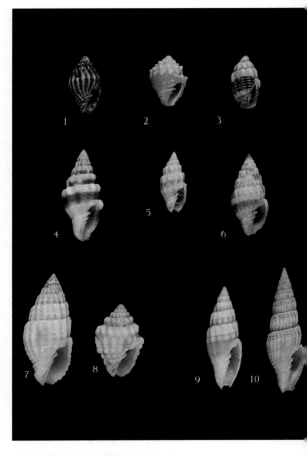

Figure 79.
Costellariidae:
Vexillum lenhilli
Kay 1979, 6 mm.

54

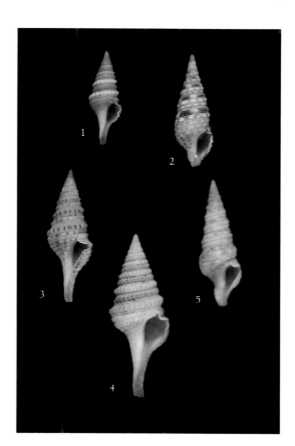

Figure 80.
Turridae:
1. *Gemmula monilifera*
(Pease, 1861), 12 mm;
2. *Xenuroturris kingae*
Powell, 1964, 20 mm;
3. *Gemmula interpolata*
Powell, 1967, 20 mm;
4. *Turris crispa intricata*
Powell, 1964, 45 mm;
5. *Xenuroturris*
gemmuloides
Powell, 1967, 20 mm.

Figure 81.
Turridae:
Daphnella interrupta
Pease, 1860, 7 mm.

Figure 82.
Conidae:
1. *Conus striatus*
Linnaeus, 1758, 80 mm;
2. *Conus textile*
Linnaeus, 1758, 80 mm;
3. *Conus vexillum*
Gmelin, 1791, 85 mm;
4. *Conus spiceri*
Bartsch and Rehder,
1943, 90 mm;
5. *Conus quercinus*
Lightfoot, 1786, 70 mm;
6. *Conus distans*
Hwass *in* Bruguiére,
1972, 90 mm.

Figure 83.
Conidae:
Conus sponsalis
Hwass *in* Bruguiére,
1792, 15 mm.

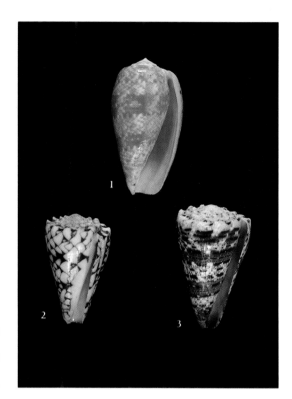

Figure 84.
Conidae:
1. *Conus bullatus*
Linnaeus, 1758, 63 mm;
2. *Conus marmoreus*
Linnaeus, 1758, 55 mm;
3. *Conus imperialis*
Linnaeus, 1758, 60 mm.

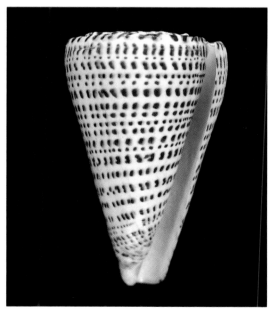

Figure 85.
Conidae:
Conus leopardus
Röding, 1798, 110 mm.

Figure 86.
Conidae:
1. *Conus litoglyphus*
Hwass *in* Bruguiére,
1792, 30 mm;
2. *Conus pertusus*
Hwass *in* Bruguiére,
1792, 25 mm;
3. *Conus nussatella*
Linnaeus, 1758, 32 mm;
4. *Conus moreleti*
Crosse, 1858, 48 mm;
5. *Conus pulicarius*
Hwass *in* Bruguiére,
1792, 48 mm;
6. *Conus vitulinus*
Hwass *in* Bruguiére,
1792, 45 mm;
7. *Conus miles*
Linnaeus 1758, 40 mm.

Figure 87.
Conidae:
Conus pertusus Hwass *in*
Bruguiére, 1792,
25 mm, with siphon
extended.

Figure 88.
Conidae:
1. *Conus abbreviatus*
Reeve, 1843, 25 mm,
2. *Conus catus*
Hwass *in* Bruguiére,
1792, 35 mm,
3. *Conus chaldaeus*
(Röding, 1798), 30 mm,
4. *Conus ebraeus*
Linnaeus, 1758, 35 mm,
5. *Conus flavidus*
Lamarck, 1810, 38 mm,
6. *Conus lividus*
Hwass *in* Bruguiére,
1792, 45 mm,
7. *Conus pennaceus*
Born, 1780, 50 mm,
8. *Conus rattus*
Hwass *in* Bruguiére,
1792, 35 mm,
9. *Conus retifer*
Menke, 1829, 40 mm.

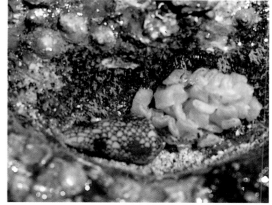

Figure 89.
Conidae:
Conus pennaceus Born,
1780, 40 mm, with egg
mass.

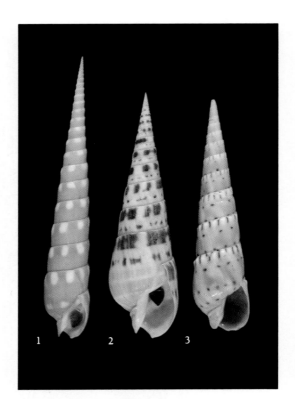

Figure 90.
Terebridae:
1. *Terebra guttata*
(Röding, 1798),
120 mm;
2. *Terebra maculata*
(Linnaeus, 1758),
105 mm;
3. *Terebra crenulata*
(Linnaeus, 1758),
100 mm.

Figure 91.
Terebridae:
Terenolla pygmaea
(Hinds, 1844), 13 mm.

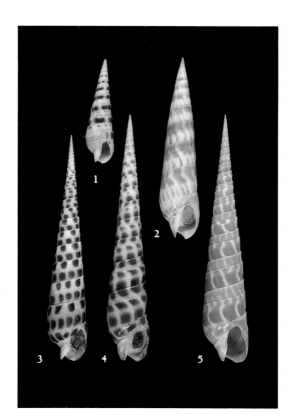

Figure 92.
Terebridae:
1. *Terebra felina*
(Dillwyn, 1817), 50 mm;
2. *Terebra chlorata*
Lamarck, 1822, 80 mm;
3. *Terebra achates*
Weaver, 1960, 100 mm;
4. *Terebra areolata*
(Link, 1807), 110 mm;
5. *Terebra dimidiata*
(Linnaeus, 1758),
110 mm.

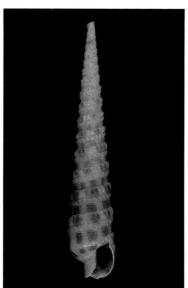

Figure 93.
Terebridae:
Terebra waikikiensis
Pilsbry, 1921, 20 mm.

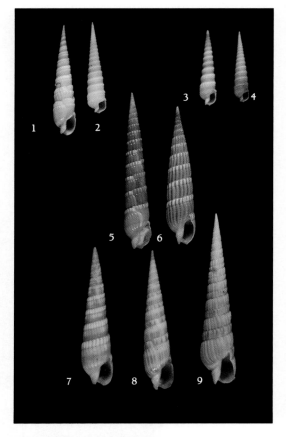

Figure 94.
Terebridae:
1. *Terebra argus brachygyra*
Pilsbry, 1921, 35 mm;
2. *Terebra nodularis*
Déshayes, 1859, 30 mm;
3. *Terebra amanda*
Hinds, 1844, 25 mm;
4. *Terebra funiculata*
Hinds, 1844, 35 mm;
5. *Terebra columellaris*
Hinds, 1844, 50 mm;
6. *Terebra undulata*
Gray, 1834, 37 mm;
7. *Terebra affinis*
Gray, 1834, 45 mm;
8. *Terebra gouldi*
Déshayes, 1859, 45 mm;
9. *Terebra thaanumi*
Pilsbry, 1921, 54 mm.

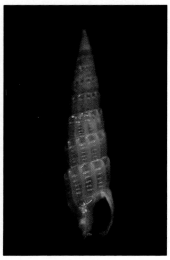

Figure 95.
Terebridae:
Terebra swainsoni
Déshayes, 1859, 30 mm.

Figure 96.
Terebridae:
1. *Hastula lanceata*
(Linnaeus, 1767),
40 mm;
2. *Hastula penicillata*
(Hinds, 1844), 30 mm;
3. *Terebra cerithina*
Lamarck, 1822, 30 mm;
4. *Hastula inconstans*
(Hinds, 1844), 32 mm;
5. *Hastula nitida*
(Hinds, 1844), 25 mm;
6. *Terebra strigilata*
(Linnaeus, 1758),
30 mm;
7. *Hastula hectica*
(Linnaeus, 1758),
45 mm;
8. *Terebra plumbea*
Quoy and Gaimard,
1833, 20 mm;
9. *Hastula matheroniana*
(Déshayes, 1859),
20 mm;
10. *Terebra swainsoni*
(Déshayes, 1859),
20 mm.

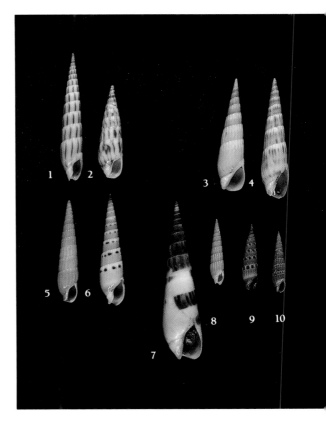

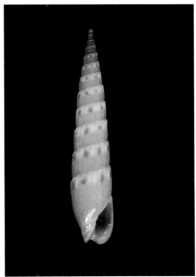

Figure 97.
Terebridae:
Hastula mera
(Hinds, 1844), 20 mm.

Figure 98.
Pyramidellidae:
1. *Otopleura mitralis*
A. Adams, 1854,
22 mm;
2. *Pyramidella dolabrata*
(Linnaeus, 1758),
25 mm;
3. *Pyramidella sulcata*
A. Adams, 1854,
25 mm.
Atyidae:
4. *Atys semistriata*
Pease, 1860, 13 mm;
5. *Atys debilis*
Pease, 1860. 15 mm.
Actaeonidae:
6. *Pupa tessellata*
(Reeve, 1842), 18 mm.
Volvatellidae:
7. *Volvatella pyriformis*
Pease, 1868, 7 mm.

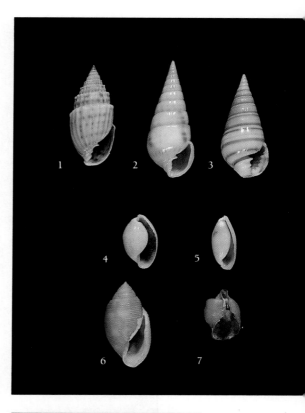

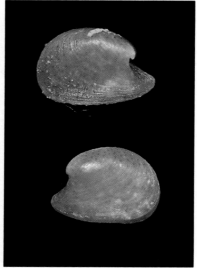

Figure 99.
Juliidae:
Julia exquisita
Gould, 1862, 3.5 mm.

Figure 100.
Volvatellidae:
Volvatella pyriformis
Pease, 1868, 10 mm.

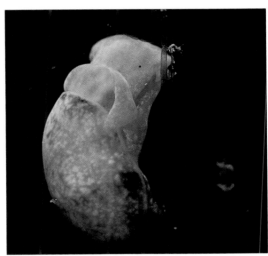

Figure 101.
Bullidae:
Bulla vernicosa
Gould, 1859,
25 mm.

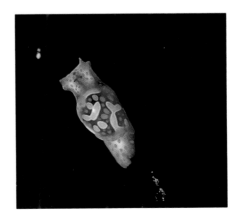

Figure 102.
Atyidae:
Haminoea cymbalum
(Quoy and Gaimard,
1835), 15 mm.

Figure 103.
Aplustridae:
Hydatina amplustre
(Linnaeus, 1758),
20 mm. (Photograph by
S. A. Reed)

Figure 104.
Aplustridae:
Hydatina physis
(Linnaeus, 1758), with
egg mass, 25 mm.

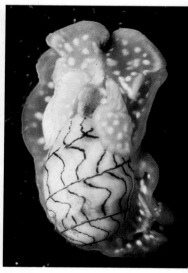

Figure 105.
Aplustridae:
Micromelo guamensis
(Quoy and Gaimard,
1825), 10 mm.

Figure 106.
Pleurobranchidae:
Euselenops luniceps
(Cuviér, 1817),
60 mm.

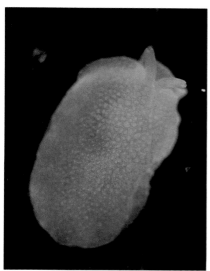

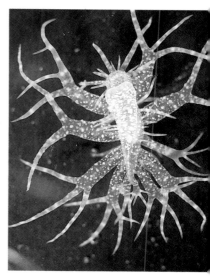

Figure 107.
Pleurobranchidae:
Pleurobranchus peronii
(Cuviér, 1804), 25 mm.

Figure 108.
Tethyidae:
Melibe megaceras
(Gosliner, 1988),
30 mm.

Figure 109.
Aplysiidae:
Aplysia oculifera
Adams and Reeve, 1850,
60 mm.

Figure 110.
Aplysiidae:
Aplysia parvula
Guilding *in* Morch,
1863, in catena, 15 mm.

Figure 111.
Aplysiidae:
Dolabrifera dolabrifera
(Rang, 1828),
35 mm.

Figure 112.
Plakobranchidae:
Elysia lobata
(Gould, 1852),
15 mm.

Figure 113.
Plakobranchidae:
Plakobranchus ocellatus
van Hasselt, 1824,
30 mm.

Figure 114.
Caliphyllidae:
Cyerce cf. *elegans*
Bergh, 1888,
30 mm.

Figure 115.
Hexabranchidae:
Hexabranchus sanguineus
(Rüppell and Leuckart,
1831), 150 mm
(Photograph by
John E. Randall)

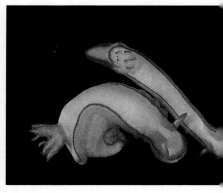

Figure 117.
Dorididae:
Hypselodoris daniellae
Kay and Young, 1969,
30 mm.

Figure 116.
Dorididae:
Chromodoris aspersa
(Gould, 1852),
30 mm.

Figure 118.
Polyceridae:
Kalinga ornata
Alder and Hancock,
1864, 100 mm.

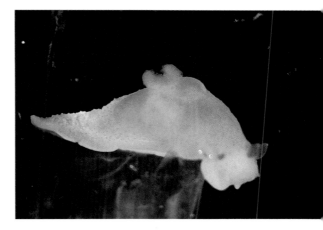

Figure 119.
Polyceridae:
Gymnodoris okinawae
Baba, 1936, 20 mm.

Figure 120.
Arminidae:
Dermatobranchus rubida
Gould, 1852, 60 mm.

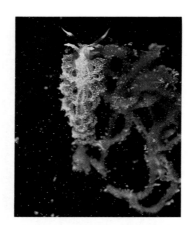

Figure 121.
Facelinidae:
Favorinus japonicus
Baba, 1949, 10 mm.

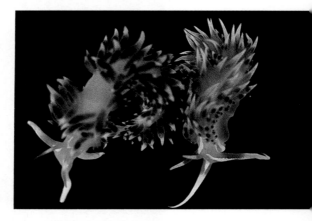

Figure 122.
Facelinidae:
Caloria militaris
(Alder and Hancock,
1866), 20 mm.

Figure 123.
Aeolidiidae;
Spurilla japonica
(Eliot, 1913),
20 mm. (Photograph
by William P. Mull)

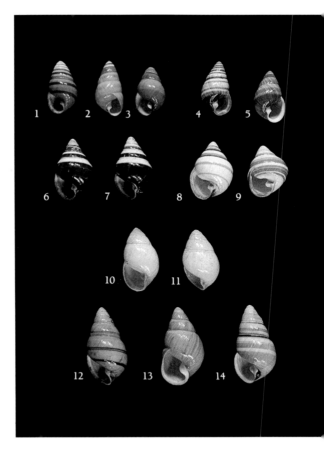

Figure 124.
Achatinellinae:
1, 2, 3. *Achatinella
sowerbyana*
Pfeiffer, 1855, 20 mm;
4, 5. *Achatinella decipiens*
Newcomb, 1853,
20 mm;
6, 7. *Achatinella
mustelina*
Mighels, 1845, 20 mm;
8, 9. *Achatinella
apexfulva*
Dixon, 1798, 23 mm;
10, 11. *Achatinella rosea*
Swainson, 1828,
25 mm;
12, 13, 14. *Achatinella
stewarti producta*
Reeve, 1850, 30 mm.

Figure 125.
Achatinellinae:
Achatinella mustelina
Mighels, 1845, 20 mm.

73

Figure 126.
Amastridae:
1. *Amastra textilis*
(Férussac, 1824),
18 mm;
2. *Amastra hutchinsoni*
(Pease, 1862), 24 mm;
3. *Amastra cylindrica*
(Newcomb, 1853),
18 mm;
4. *Laminella gravida*
(Férussac, 1824),
24 mm;
5. *Carelia sinclairi*
Ancey, 1892, 30 mm;
6. *Amastra nucleola*
(Gould, 1845), 11 mm;
7. *Amastra obesa*
(Newcomb, 1853),
13 mm;
8. *Amastra turritella*
(Férussac, 1824),
16 mm;
9. *Laminella sanguinea*
(Newcomb, 1853),
20 mm;
10, 11. *Carelia bicolor*
(Jay, 1839), 35 mm;
12. *Carelia cochlea*
(Reeve, 1849), 38 mm.

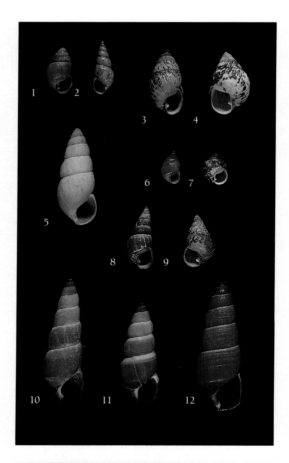

Figure 127.
Amastridae:
Laminella sanguinea
(Newcomb, 1853),
20 mm. (Photograph by
William P. Mull)

Figure 128.
Arcidae:
1. *Barbatia (Acar)
divaricata*
(Sowerby, 1833),
28 mm;
2. *Arca kauaia*
(Dall, Bartsch, and
Rehder, 1938),
22 mm;
3. *Barbatia rectangula*
(Dall, Bartsch, and
Rehder, 1938),
27 mm;
4. *Arca ventricosa*
Lamarck, 1819, 44 mm;
5. *Barbatia tenella*
(Reeve, 1844), 42 mm.
Mytilidae:
6. *Amygdalum peasei*
(Newcomb, 1870),
27 mm.
Pteriidae:
7. *Pteria brunnea*
(Pease, 1863), 27 mm.
Glycymerididae:
8. *Glycymeris
arcodentiens*
(Dall, 1895), 28 mm.

Figure 129.
Pteriidae:
Pteria brunnea
(Pease, 1863), 25 mm,
attached to black coral.

75

Figure 130.
Pinnidae:
1. *Atrina vexillum*
(Born, 1798),
125 mm;
2. *Streptopinna saccata*
(Linnaeus, 1758),
125 mm;
3. *Pinna muricata*
Linnaeus, 1758,
125 mm.

Figure 131.
Pinnidae:
Bed of *Pinna bicolor*
Gmelin, 1791,
at 30 m depth.
(Photograph by
John Maciolek)

Figure 132.
Isognomonidae:
1. *Isognomon perna*
(Linnaeus, 1767),
37 mm;
2. *Isognomon legumen*
(Gmelin, 1791), 45 mm;
3. *Isognomon incisum*
(Conrad, 1837), 30 mm.
Malleidae:
4. *Malleus regula*
(Forskål, 1775), 30 mm.
Isognomonidae:
5. *Isognomon
californicum*
(Conrad, 1837), 35 mm.

Figure 133.
Isognomonidae:
Isognomon perna
(Linnaeus, 1767),
30 mm.

Figure 134.
Limidae:
1. *Lima lahaina*
Dall, Bartsch, and
Rehder, 1938, 27 mm;
2. *Lima parallela*
Dall, Bartsch, and
Rehder, 1938, 20 mm;
3. *Lima keokeo*
Dall, Bartsch, and
Rehder, 1938, 27 mm.
Pectinidae:
4. *Pecten waikikius*
Dall, Bartsch, and
Rehder, 1938, 15 mm;
5. *Chlamys irregularis*
(Sowerby, 1842),
20 mm;
6, 7. *Haumea juddi*
Dall, Bartsch, and
Rehder, 1938, 15 mm;
8. *Mirapecten mirificus*
(Reeve, 1853), 17 mm;
9. *Decatopecten
noduliferum*
(Sowerby, 1842),
23 mm.
Anomiidae:
10. *Anomia nobilis*
Reeve, 1859, 35 mm.
Pectinidae:
11. *Cryptopecten bullatus*
(Dautzenberg and
Bavay, 1912), 39 mm.

Figure 135.
Limidae:
Lima fragilis Chemnitz,
1784, 30 mm.
(Photograph by Chris
Takahashi)

Figure 136.
Lucinidae:
1. *Lucina edentula*
(Linnaeus, 1758),
20 mm.
Veneridae:
2. *Lioconcha
hieroglyphica*
(Conrad, 1837), 30 mm;
3. *Ctena bella*
(Conrad, 1837), 20 mm;
4. *Venus toreuma*
Gould, 1850, 24 mm;
5. *Codakia punctata*
(Linnaeus, 1758),
35 mm;
6. *Periglypta reticulata*
(Linnaeus, 1758),
40 mm.
Cardiidae:
7. *Trachycardium orbita*
(Sowerby, 1833),
40 mm.
Trapeziidae:
8. *Trapezium oblongum*
(Linnaeus, 1758),
40 mm.

Figure 137.
Veneridae:
Periglypta reticulata
(Linnaeus, 1758), 50
mm, with siphons
protruding.

Figure 138.
Tellinidae:
1. *Tellina crucigera*
Lamarck, 1818, 50 mm;
2. *Tellina perna*
(Spengler, 1798),
80 mm;
3. *Tellina elizabethae*
Pilsbry, 1918, 40 mm;
4. *Tellina palatam*
Iredale, 1929, 60 mm.

Figure 139.
Tellinidae:
Tellina perna
(Spengler, 1798), 65
mm, with siphons
protruding.

Figure 140.
Tellinidae:
1. *Tellina robusta*
(Hanley, 1844), 12 mm.
Semelidae:
2. *Semelangulus*
crebrimaculatus
Sowerby, 1867, 15 mm.
Tellinidae:
3. *Tellina hawaiensis*
Dall, Bartsch, and
Rehder, 1938, 25 mm;
4. *Macoma dispar*
(Conrad, 1837), 20 mm.
Mactridae:
5. *Mactra thaanumi*
Dall, Bartsch, and
Rehder, 1938, 10 mm.
Cardiidae:
6. *Nemocardium*
thaanumi
(Pilsbry, 1921), 10 mm.
Glossidae:
7. *Meiocardia hawaiana*
Dall, Bartsch, and
Rehder, 1938, 25 mm.
Cardiidae:
8. *Fragum mundum*
(Reeve, 1845), 9 mm.

Figure 141.
Spondylidae:
Spondylus linguaefelis
Sowerby, 1847, 80 mm,
at 46.1 m (140 feet)
depth, Molokini off
Maui. (Photograph by
Mike Severns)

References

Bertsch, H., and S. Johnson. 1981. *Hawaiian Nudibranchs.* Oriental Publishing Company, Honolulu, Hawaii.

Ford, J. I., and R. A. Kinzie III. 1982. Life crawls upstream. *Natural History* 91:60–67.

Hadfield, M. G. 1986. Extinction in Hawaiian achatinelline snails. *Malacologia* 27:67–81.

Hadfield, M. G., and S. E. Miller. 1989. Demographic studies of *Partulina proxima. Pacific Science* 43:1–16.

Hadfield, M. G., and B. S. Mountain. 1981. A field study of a vanishing species, *Achatinella mustelina* (Gastropoda, Pulmonata), in the Waianae Mountains of Oahu. *Pacific Science* 34:345–358.

Hopper, C. N. 1981. The ecology and reproductive biology of some Hawaiian vermetid gastropods. Ph.D. dissertation, University of Hawaii, Honolulu, Hawaii.

Kay, E. A. 1967. The composition and relationships of marine molluscan fauna of the Hawaiian Islands. *Venus* 25:96–104.

———. 1979. *Hawaiian Marine Shells.* B. P. Bishop Museum Press, Honolulu, Hawaii.

Kay, E. A. and S. R. Palumbi. 1987. Endemism and evolution in Hawaiian marine invertebrates. *Trends in Evolution and Ecology* 2:183–186.

Kohn, A. J. 1959. The ecology of *Conus* in Hawaii. *Ecological Monographs* 29:47–90.

Sarver, D. 1977. The ecology and energetics of *Aplysia juliana* (Quoy and Gaimard, 1832). Ph.D. dissertation, University of Hawaii, Honolulu, Hawaii.

Taylor, J. B. 1975. Planktonic prosobranch veligers of Kaneohe Bay. Ph.D. dissertation, University of Hawaii, Honolulu, Hawaii.

Van Heukelem, W. F. 1966. Growth and life span of *Octopus cyanea* (Mollusca: Cephalopoda). *Zoological Journal London* 169:299–315.

Index of Scientific Names

Family names begin with capital letters and end in "dae." Generic and species names are italicized. Generic names are capitalized; species names are not capitalized.

85

About the Authors

E. Alison Kay is professor of zoology at the University of Hawaii, where she has taught since 1957. A graduate of Mills College, Cambridge University, and the University of Hawaii, she has made mollusks a specialty and has written extensively about them as well as about the natural history of the Hawaiian Islands. Other books by her include *Hawaiian Marine Shells* and *A Natural History of the Hawaiian Islands,* the mollusk section of *Reef and Shore Fauna of Hawaii,* and *Marine Mollusca of the Cuming Collection.*

Olive Schoenberg-Dole, a graduate of the University of California (Berkeley), also attended the University of Hawaii. She has combined her interest in photography and malacology to become a well-known contributor of shell photographs to numerous publications. Her work has appeared in *Hawaiian Shell News, Hawaiian Marine Mollusks, Kingdom of the Seashell,* and *Cowries of the World.* She has also developed a slideshow titled "Molluscan Camouflage."